Henry VII

D1333499

IN THE SAME SERIES

General Editors: Eric J. Evans and P.D. King

LANCASTER PAMPHLETS

Henry VII

The importance of his reign
in English history

Alexander Grant

London and New York

First published in 1985 by
Methuen & Co. Ltd

Reprinted 1989, 1992, 1996
by Routledge
11 New Fetter Lane,
London EC4P 4EE
29 West 35th Street,
New York NY 10001

All rights reserved. No part of this
book may be reprinted or reproduced
or utilized in any form or by any
electronic, mechanical or other means,
now known or hereafter invented,
including photocopying and recording,
or in any information storage or
retrieval system, without permission in
writing from the publishers.

© 1985 Alexander Grant

British Library Cataloguing in
Publication Data

Grant, Alexander, 1947–
Henry VII: the importance of his
reign in English history – (Lancaster
pamphlets)
1. Great Britain – History – Henry
VII, 1485–1509
I. Title   II. Series
942.05'1   DA330

ISBN 0–415–04037–X

Typeset in Great Britain by
Scarborough Typesetting Services
and printed in England by
Clays Ltd, St Ives plc

Contents

Foreword

Lancaster Pamphlets offer concise and up-to-date accounts of major historical topics, primarily for the help of students preparing for Advanced Level examinations, though they should also be of value to those pursuing introductory courses in universities and other institutions of higher education. They do not rely on prior textbook knowledge. Without being all-embracing, their aims are to bring some of the central themes or problems confronting students and teachers into sharper focus than the textbook writer can hope to do; to provide the reader with some of the results of recent research which the textbook may not embody; and to stimulate thought about the whole interpretation of the topic under discussion.

At the end of this pamphlet is a list of the recent or fairly recent works that the writer considers most relevant to the subject.

Acknowledgement

My colleagues Eric Evans and David King performed their editorial tasks of encouraging, criticizing and chivvying a laggard author with exemplary efficiency and patience; my warmest thanks to them both.

Note

References. A number in brackets in the text indicates reference to a work in the 'Further reading' section.

Money. It is virtually impossible to express medieval and early modern sums of money in modern values, but, since in the fifteenth century £5–£10 a year was a comfortable income, it is likely that the money of Henry VII's reign could be multiplied by between 1000 and 2000 times to bring it roughly into line with present (mid-1980s) values. Thus a sum of £1000 in Henry's reign would probably be worth somewhere between £1,000,000 and £2,000,000 nowadays.

Henry VII

The importance of his reign in English history

Introduction

This pamphlet was written in 1985, the year which marks the five hundredth anniversary of Henry Tudor's seizure of the English throne from Richard III at the battle of Bosworth. For most of those five hundred years this event, the accession of the first Tudor monarch, has been regarded as one of the major turning-points in English history; and, indeed, that idea is reflected nowadays in the fact that history courses are still commonly devoted to 'the Tudors' or 'the Tudors and Stewarts', especially in schools. Yet, at the same time, the standard academic view of Henry VII attaches relatively little significance to his being the first of the Tudors. The traditional 'turning-point' view has been almost entirely discredited; continuity with his Yorkist predecessors, especially Edward IV, is widely considered to be the main characteristic of the reign. The result is to make 1485 an extremely awkward starting-point, especially for those who have not studied the period previously.

During the last ten years or so, however, the strength of what we can call the 'continuity thesis' about Henry's reign has been weakened by a substantial amount of new research, especially that by Professor Charles Ross on Edward IV. In Professor Ross's view, Edward IV 'should not be too readily regarded as a Mk I version of Henry VII. The difference in their personalities is

1

profound, and the differences between their policies are hardly less important than the resemblances' (22). Other recent work, too, indicates that there was much more of a break between Henry VII and his Yorkist predecessors than the current textbook orthodoxy would allow. Indeed, when the differences between Edward IV's and Henry VII's kingship are put into a long-term perspective, then a case can be made for regarding Henry VII's accession as a most important turning-point after all – and certainly as a sensible point for beginning a period of English history.

Any discussion of the place of Henry VII's reign in English history must start by looking at it in relation to the 'Wars of the Roses' – the sequence of civil wars which broke out in 1455 and lasted until Henry defeated the forces of the Yorkist pretender Lambert Simnel at the battle of Stoke in 1487. It is, of course, generally agreed that Henry's two victories, first at Bosworth and then at Stoke, brought the civil wars to an end. Yet the current orthodoxy tends to play down the seriousness of these wars, their coherence as a continuous conflict and the significance of their ending.

Recent studies, however, show that this is a mistake. Various points could be made about the Wars of the Roses, but here there is only space to stress the main one: that from the 1450s to the 1480s the English crown was far more vulnerable than at any time since the Norman Conquest. Henry VII's four predecessors – Henry VI, Edward IV, Edward V and Richard III – all lost their thrones, in three cases permanently; during the period the crown changed hands violently no fewer than five times; and there were also several unsuccessful rebellions and attempted *coups d'état*. Successful or unsuccessful, the rebellions and *coups d'état* were all stimulated, in the last resort, by the fact that it seemed remarkably easy to unseat the king; in this period, indeed, England appears very similar to the notoriously unstable states of Latin America in modern times. It is this instability, sparked off by the rebellions of Richard duke of York (Edward IV's father) in the 1450s and lasting until Henry VII's reign, which gives the main coherence and significance to the concept of the Wars of the Roses.

Now, admittedly, Henry VII's accession did not restore stability to England overnight. After Bosworth the battle of

2

Stoke still had to be fought; after Stoke there were other 'Yorkist' conspiracies; and after Henry VII's death the legacy of instability lingered on under Henry VIII. What was at times a near-paranoid concern for security was, indeed, one of the main characteristics of the reigns of the first two Tudors. Nevertheless, the vital point is that, in striking contrast to his predecessors, Henry VII *did* keep his throne. There may have been rebellions and conspiracies after 1485, but that was when the last *successful* one took place. After 1485 – after Henry VII's accession – all rebellions and conspiracies were crushed. So, despite the Tudors' worries about security (or perhaps, as we shall see, partly because of them), it is clear with hindsight that after Henry Tudor became king the English crown ceased to be so vulnerable. In view of the political upheavals of the period before 1485, this point can hardly be emphasized enough.

The military factor

It is one thing to emphasize that with Henry VII's reign a much higher degree of political stability was established in England, quite another to explain why that happened. There is no one straightforward answer to that question; instead, a variety of factors needs to be examined.

To begin with, we must consider military affairs; the throne had to be won in 1485 and defended thereafter. Although Henry VII is not renowned as a warrior king, he did in fact have a very good military record. In 1485, for example, the campaign leading up to Bosworth was quick and decisive; he led his forces from Milford Haven in Pembrokeshire into Leicestershire, in the heart of England, in less than a fortnight, so giving Richard III as little time as possible to react. And while what happened in the actual battle is not entirely clear, recent studies indicate (20, 23) that the Tudor army took the field very early in the morning, and caught Richard III's forces at a distinct disadvantage. Admittedly the eventual victory came when part of the Stanley forces, which had been watching on the sidelines, joined in on Henry's side. But that was not simply luck. First, Lord Stanley was Henry's stepfather (the third husband of

Henry's mother Margaret Beaufort), and Henry had been in close contact with him before and after invading England; Henry was clearly relying on Stanley support. The Stanleys' treachery to Richard was not, therefore, unexpected; possibly the only surprise for Henry was the unpleasant one that they did not commit themselves until the battle was well under way. Second, when the Stanleys did join in it was probably because they saw the battle was going Henry's way. Earlier Henry's vanguard had engaged Richard's, had driven it back and had killed its commander. That was crucial, because it made Richard decide on his desperate, poorly supported cavalry charge against Henry's personal position – and it was that which persuaded the Stanleys to join what almost certainly appeared to be the winning side. The victory at Bosworth, therefore, should be attributed as much to the successes of Henry's own forces as to the Stanley intervention. (A comment is needed here on the military significance of the Stanleys. Since the early fifteenth century they had been the dominant local family in Cheshire and south Lancashire, an area which throughout the later middle ages had been one of the main suppliers of troops for English armies. As a result they probably had larger and more experienced forces at their disposal than almost any of the other English magnates.)

Similarly, subsequent military challenges to Henry's rule were dealt with by speedy, intelligent and effective action. Although some historians state that the one other battle of the reign, at Stoke (near Newark, Lincolnshire) in 1487 was a near thing, that is not true. In fact, the royal army dealt with its opponents, the forces supporting Lambert Simnel and John de la Pole, earl of Lincoln, quite comfortably – 'without deaths of any noble or gentleman on our part', as Henry himself put it. Only part of Henry's army needed to fight at Stoke; not, as has been suggested, because the rest was untrustworthy, but because, just as at Bosworth, Henry deliberately entrusted the main brunt of the fighting to his vanguard, while he himself stayed sensibly (and this time safely) in the rear. The vanguard clearly consisted of an elite force, based on Henry's household and led by good, experienced commanders [20], in particular John de Vere, earl of Oxford, who commanded it at Bosworth and Stoke, and who had earlier gained one of the best military reputations among the Lancastrian leaders in the Wars of the Roses. One feature of all Henry's campaigns is that he always chose his subordinate commanders wisely – which, of course, is one of the signs of a good commander-in-chief.

Thus Henry won and kept his throne partly at least because he was successful, and probably good, at military affairs. There is a striking contrast with Richard III's ultimately suicidal behaviour at Bosworth. Also, Henry's military record contrasts significantly with Edward IV's. Edward is generally praised as a military leader, and he did win several great victories. But he also twice found himself completely outmanoeuvred by opponents – to such an extent that on both occasions his own troops deserted him. In 1469 he was captured; in 1470 he fled the country. That kind of thing never happened to Henry VII who, unlike Edward, always appears to have been in control of whatever military situation confronted him.

Internal security

Henry's success in keeping the throne is not, however, to be explained purely in military terms. Another major factor was his ability to nip conspiracies in the bud or, at worst, limit challenges to his rule; again there is a significant contrast with his predecessors. That was largely the result of a good 'intelligence service' from agents and informers (both voluntary and involuntary), and also of an acute awareness of its value. Admittedly, agents and informers did not appear overnight in 1485, yet in earlier reigns they do not seem to have been so effective. For example, Edward IV was taken completely by surprise in 1469 and 1470 by rebellions instigated by the great Richard Neville, earl of Warwick (sometimes known as 'the Kingmaker'), and by his own brother, the duke of Clarence. Richard III, similarly, did not discover about Lord Stanley's treasonable dealings with Henry Tudor until too late – and when he did, he did not take effective action. Edward IV and Richard III either failed to make the best use of the information available to them, or did not receive very good information in the first place. Both kings certainly seem to have been too complacent at crucial periods in their reigns.

Henry VII was also perhaps rather complacent to begin with. The Lambert Simnel conspiracy (in which the young son of an Oxford joiner impersonated the earl of Warwick, a nephew of the Yorkist kings) had probably been in preparation for some time before he learned about it, and when he did his intelligence was faulty, for no steps were taken against the earl of Lincoln in February 1487. Indeed, Lincoln, genuinely and menacingly Yorkist by birth, attended the meeting of the royal council which debated what to do about Simnel. When Lincoln joined Simnel, it must have been a painful blow to Henry – but one which he never suffered again. Thereafter, the activities of agents and informers are a notable feature of the reign. Henry's 'intelligence policy' is very well illustrated by a document from his son's reign, in which one of Cardinal Wolsey's agents, investigating allegations against the duke of Buckingham in 1521, reported:

> And so, if it please your grace, of likelihood some great matter there is. . . . Very good policy it were to have the truth known. The king that dead is [Henry VII] would handle such a cause circumspectly and with convenient diligence for inveigling, and yet not disclose it to the party . . . but keep it to himself, and always grope further. (29)

The value to Henry of agents and informers comes out clearly from the Perkin Warbeck affair. Warbeck claimed to be the younger of Edward IV's sons, the 'Princes in the Tower,' but details of his true identity – he was from Flanders, a son of an official in Tournai – were quickly revealed, and when a conspiracy in his favour was hatched in England in 1493 it was soon uncovered. One of the conspirators turned king's evidence (or had been in Henry's employment all along); on his information the rest of the plotters were rounded up, tried and executed or imprisoned during the winter of 1494–5. Similarly, while Warbeck was in Scotland in 1496–7, important information about his activities and English contacts was provided by a prominent Scottish noble who was in Henry's pay. None of Warbeck's attempts to invade England ever came to anything; credit for that must go at least partly to Henry's ability to collect information and make good use of it.

The most striking victim of Henry's 'intelligence service' was Sir William Stanley, the person who had brought the Stanley forces in on Henry's side at Bosworth. Sir William and his brother Thomas Lord Stanley had been well rewarded for that, and Sir William had become head of Henry's household (private staff and bodyguard). In 1494, however, he was named among those involved with Perkin Warbeck; and although all that he could be accused of was agreeing not to oppose Warbeck if Warbeck were the true son of Edward IV, that was enough to bring about his trial, conviction and execution in February 1495. Some historians have argued that Stanley – who did not have the benefit of hindsight – was simply taking out a sensible insurance against a further change of dynasty. But that misses the point. Henry VII, unlike his predecessors, was not prepared to tolerate Stanley ambivalence. The fact that he would not take the risk of a repetition of Sir William Stanley's treachery towards Richard III helps to explain why he succeeded in keeping the throne for his own dynasty. Stanley's lack of absolute loyalty would have been doubly alarming in view of the fact that the household provided the essential core of the royal army.

The other main victim of Henry's concern for security was the much more tragic figure of Edward earl of Warwick. Warwick was the son of Edward IV's treacherous brother, the duke of Clarence (who had been put to death in 1478). Soon after Henry VII's accession, Warwick (then only ten years old) was imprisoned in the Tower of London; he stayed there for the rest of his life. In the Tower Warwick was hardly a threat to Henry, but things might have been different had he escaped, given that he was a true member of the Yorkist royal family, in contrast to the pretenders Simnel and Warbeck. At any rate, shortly after Perkin Warbeck joined him in the Tower in 1498, Henry's agents discovered – or perhaps fabricated – a plot to free both of them. Warwick was duly charged with treasonable conspiracy, which he admitted, and he was beheaded in November 1499; Perkin Warbeck was hanged two days later.

There was, of course, nothing new about executing magnates in fifteenth-century England; indeed, many more of them went to the scaffold under Henry VI or Edward IV than under Henry VII. But the executions in the previous reigns were all carried out by the victorious party in the aftermath of rebellions and *coups d'état*; there seems to be no immediate precedent for such cold-blooded 'pre-emptive strikes' as the executions of the earl of Warwick and Sir William Stanley. These can be called 'precautionary executions' – executions intended to deal with trouble *before* it took place rather than afterwards. As such they indicate a much more acute concern for security than Edward IV exhibited. And that is something which characterizes the reign as a whole. Henry's concern for security has been interpreted by some historians as reflecting a basic *insecurity* in his regime. But it would be more apt to say that he was not prepared to take any chances at all of suffering the experiences of his four predecessors. The result may well have been to make him obsessively conscious of security. On the other hand, that also goes a long way towards explaining why Henry VII, in contrast to his predecessors, was ultimately successful in keeping the throne for himself and for his dynasty.

The royal family

Another of the reasons why the throne did not change hands violently after 1485 is that Henry VII's regime was not seriously weakened at its very heart by the affairs of the immediate royal family, in the way that the Yorkist regime had been. Before 1485, indeed, rivalries and quarrels within the royal family had been largely responsible for destabilizing and, in the end, destroying Yorkist kingship; but they did not weaken Henry VII's kingship at all.

In the first part of Edward IV's reign, for instance, resentment against his queen, Elizabeth Woodville, and her grasping kindred was one of the main grievances which turned both Richard Neville, earl of Warwick, and Edward's brother, the duke of Clarence, against the king in 1469–70. Then, after Edward's restoration in 1471 (when Neville was killed), Clarence stupidly continued to cause trouble, until at last Edward had to have him put to death for 'incorrigible treason' in 1478. Third, when Edward himself died in 1483, the usurpation of his young son's throne by his other brother, Richard duke of Gloucester – Richard III – is at least partly explicable in terms of Yorkist family politics. Many of those who supported Gloucester's *coup d'état*, especially in its early stages, did so out of hatred for the Woodville kindred, who had dominated the affairs of the young king when he had been prince of Wales. Some, too, had a vested interest in the downfall of both of Edward IV's sons, because Edward IV had unjustly manipulated the descent of the great inheritance of the Mowbray dukes of Norfolk into the hands of his younger son. And Edward IV made matters worse for his sons by giving Richard of Gloucester huge grants of land and authority in the north of England, without doing anything to reconcile Gloucester and the Woodvilles.

The result was the disaster of 1483 when, on Edward's death, the hostilities within his family circle exploded, culminating in Richard III's usurpation and his murder of his young nephews. That undid the achievements of the second part of Edward's reign and, indeed, shattered the Yorkist regime, preparing the way for Henry Tudor's successful invasion two years later. Up to June 1483 Henry Tudor was hardly any more plausible as a potential king of England than Lambert Simnel or Perkin Warbeck were to be later. It was the devastating effect that Richard III's usurpation had on the Yorkist regime that gave Henry his opportunity. Many of Edward's closest supporters, in fact, fled to Henry Tudor; in some ways Bosworth was a 'Yorkist revenge' on Richard III. That clearly brings out the extreme importance of family politics in Yorkist England.

In Henry VII's reign things were completely different. Whereas, for example, Edward IV's marriage to Elizabeth Woodville was a disastrous mistake, Henry VII's to Elizabeth of York was the most sensible marriage possible. It was designed to heal political divisions, and probably did so. But after it, the queen and her relatives (who could be called Woodvilles, since Elizabeth of York was the daughter of Elizabeth Woodville) were kept in the background, so far as politics were concerned. Woodville influence, or the influence of the queen's relatives, was no longer a factor in the England of Henry VII. Moreover, unlike Edward IV, Henry VII had no brothers to cause problems either during his reign or after his death. He did have two sons, but Arthur died in 1502 aged only fifteen, while the young Henry was only seventeen at the end of the reign; thus neither son was a major political

9

figure. Apart from his sons, Henry VII's closest male relatives were his two uncles. But one of these, Viscount Welles, was a fairly insignificant person who hardly ever featured in national affairs. The other, Jasper Tudor, duke of Bedford, was an extremely prominent magnate; but he had been the main upholder of the Tudor cause before 1485, he was completely loyal to Henry, his main interests were in Wales and, most significantly, he died childless in 1495. Henry's mother, Margaret countess of Richmond, was also a major landowner in her own right, but she too was absolutely loyal. And so, despite his suspect record before 1485, was her third husband, Henry VII's step-father, Thomas Lord Stanley (created earl of Derby in 1485). Admittedly his brother, Sir William Stanley, was executed for treason in 1495, but that is the only time that political problems ever arose even on the fringe of Henry's family circle.

Of course the fact that Henry had so few close relatives was not part of his deliberate policy. But even if he had had a large family, it is unlikely that he would have treated it as generously as Edward IV treated his. That is clear, to begin with, from the way in which his queen was kept in the background, and also from the fact that he endowed her with land worth only about two-thirds as much as Elizabeth Woodville had received from Edward IV. Similarly, although Jasper Tudor was given the title of duke and quite a large amount of land, especially in Wales, he had nothing like the grants Edward IV gave to his brothers, Clarence and Gloucester. And, most strikingly, consider the ways the two kings treated their younger sons. Both were made dukes of York and (although under age) were given another large inheritance to augment the lands of that duchy: the inheritance of the Mowbray dukes of Norfolk was diverted to Edward IV's son, while the estates left by Jasper Tudor in 1495 were given to the young Henry. But whereas Edward IV's son, although a minor, appears to have received the revenues from these estates, Henry VII kept the revenues of his younger son's lands in his own hands. Moreover when after Arthur's death young Henry became prince of Wales, he was made to surrender the duchy of York and Jasper Tudor's lands, on the grounds that the traditional estates of the prince (the principality of Wales, duchy of Cornwall and earldom

10

of Chester) were sufficient for him. But again the revenues were withheld from him and paid directly into Henry VII's own coffers. Thus, whereas Edward IV manipulated other nobles' inheritances to the benefit of his younger son, Henry VII manipulated his younger son's endowment to benefit himself. That epitomizes the difference between the two reigns.

Now it has been commented that when Henry VII made his younger son duke of York he was creating a junior branch of the royal family that was potentially as dangerous as earlier houses of York, Lancaster or most recently Gloucester had been. But the lands of the duchy of York were worth less than £1000 a year, which in the middle ages was regarded as the minimum income for an earl. Jasper Tudor's estates added about another £2000 in yearly revenue, but they mostly lay in Wales. Thus the lands and power base in England allocated to young Henry as duke of York (had he ever received them) were not nearly as extensive as those of previous dukes of York, Lancaster and Gloucester. It is most unlikely that his estates would have made him an 'overmighty' threat to his brother, had Arthur lived and succeeded to the throne (although his personality might have done).

But of course that argument is hypothetical, because Arthur did die, young Henry became king and no junior branch of the Tudor royal family was established. In contrast to the Yorkists, indeed, the family problems of the Tudor monarchs derived from the fact that their immediate families were small, not large. And as far as Henry VII is concerned, the point is that, as has been aptly remarked, 'unlike the situation under Edward IV, there was no centre within the king's kindred for rival political tensions and no obvious focus for political discontent' (9). Because of that, the opportunity given to Henry Tudor in 1485 was *not* presented to subsequent Yorkist pretenders. They faced a relatively united regime, not one shattered by family hostilities.

The nobility

We must now turn to the rest of the nobility. The traditional view, that the old 'overmighty' nobility of late medieval England killed itself off in the Wars of the Roses, has been shown to be

11

false. The direct male lines of peerage families did not, in fact, become extinct more frequently in the Wars of the Roses period than earlier or later. In almost every twenty-five-year generation during the fourteenth, fifteenth and sixteenth centuries, no less than a quarter of the peers failed to leave sons to succeed them. This very high extinction rate caused a rapid turnover in noble families. So there were always 'new' families around in every generation; the Tudor nobility was no 'newer' than what went before. This, obviously, forms an important element in the current 'continuity thesis'.

These bald statistics, however, are to a certain extent misleading. They ignore the occasions when a family, although surviving, lost its peerage through forfeiture or royal displeasure. Also, more importantly, they show extinction rates only, not the rate at which extinct families were replaced. When these points are taken into consideration, then the picture becomes rather different. Analysis of the information in the *Complete Peerage* shows that under Edward IV the extinction + forfeiture rate works out at 25 per cent, while the replacement rate was 31 per cent; the peerage grew from forty-two members at the beginning of the reign to forty-six at its end. Under Henry VII, in contrast, the extinction + forfeiture rate was much higher, at 42 per cent, while the replacement rate was only 17 per cent (the reign saw only eight new creations). Thus Henry VII's peerage shrank considerably. When he became king there were fifty peers (including half a dozen restored immediately after Bosworth); when he died there were only thirty-five. The number of peers had fallen by 30 per cent. (In this analysis, kings' brothers and other kinsmen have been included, but kings' sons have not.)

At the top of the nobility, the contrast between the two reigns is even more striking. Under Edward IV the number of major peers (dukes, marquesses and earls) grew from seven to twelve, whereas under Henry VII it shrank from sixteen (including four restored at his accession) to ten. The only significant promotions to the rank of earl and above, indeed, were those of his stepfather (from Lord Stanley to earl of Derby) and his uncle (from earl of Pembroke to duke of Bedford). Henry VII's peerage was not only becoming smaller in size, but was also becoming 'smaller' with respect to the status of its members.

12

This is particularly true with respect to the near disappearance of those we may call 'super-nobles', men who combined in their own possession the inheritances of several major families. These were the 'overmighty' magnates who used to be seen as one of the great evils of medieval English political society. Recent work treats them more sympathetically, yet it should be pointed out that it was these 'super-nobles' who led the major rebellions and *coups d'état* which punctuate late medieval English political history, and their virtual absence from Henry VII's reign goes far towards explaining its relative stability.

To understand their absence, we must ask how they appeared in the first place. They were often junior members of the royal family, such as the dukes of Lancaster, York and Gloucester. But they did not only originate in the royal family. The prestige and power of Richard Neville, earl of Warwick ('the Kingmaker'), derived chiefly from his vast estates, which had come through various inheritances: from his father, the main Neville family estates; from his mother, the estates of the Montague earls of Salisbury; from his wife's father, the estates of the Beauchamp earls of Warwick; and from his wife's mother, the estates of the Despenser family. Each of these inheritances was sufficient for a substantial peer; 'Warwick the Kingmaker' enjoyed all four.

Richard Neville was by no means unique in this. Earlier, the vast territories of the dukes of Lancaster and York had been built up more through inheritance than royal grant. Or consider Humphrey Stafford. In 1444, shortly before being made duke of Buckingham, he described himself as 'the right mighty prince Humphrey earl of Buckingham, Hereford, Stafford, Northampton and Perche [in France], lord of Brecknock and Holderness' – which strikingly reflects the combination of inheritances in his possession. The late medieval English nobility was, in fact, experiencing a 'snowball effect' (25), a trend for more and more land to come into the hands of fewer and fewer landowners, leading to the emergence of 'super-nobles' at the top of the social hierarchy.

This 'snowball effect' is connected with the high extinction rate among peerage families. When direct male lines became extinct, family estates often went to female heiresses; and since they usually married into families of equal social status, the tendency was to combine estates. The possessions of Richard Neville, earl of Warwick, give a perfect example: his wife, his mother and his maternal grandmother were all major heiresses, whose inheritances greatly increased the basic Neville lands.

Richard Neville, in turn, left no sons when he was killed in 1471, and his vast estates went to his two daughters who married Edward IV's brothers, the dukes of Clarence and Gloucester. Thus the Warwick inheritance was shared between these two dukes, who were both major landowners in their own right. This is one instance of how the 'snowball effect' – and the emergence of overmighty 'super-nobles' – was continuing during Edward IV's reign. And although Clarence's challenges to Edward IV eventually caused his own downfall and death, Gloucester proved to be one of the most notorious of all late medieval England's overmighty magnates, when – with the help of another 'super-noble', Henry second duke of Buckingham – he seized the throne in 1483. The cases of Gloucester and Buckingham, incidentally, disprove the argument of some historians that there were no 'overmighty' magnates by the end of Edward IV's reign.

Overmighty magnates did *not*, however, emerge in Henry VII's reign in the same way. One reason is the absence of Henry's close relatives and his limited generosity to those he did have. There was no one to compare with the dukes of Clarence and Gloucester under Edward IV. Indeed, Clarence's lands had come into the crown's hands with his forfeiture in 1478 and his son's imprisonment in 1485, while Gloucester's lands had gone to the crown when he himself became king in 1483. This was a common pattern. When overmighty magnates challenged the crown, they were either defeated and suffered forfeiture, or were victorious and gained the throne; in both cases the crown took over their lands. But, generally, most of those lands were subsequently granted away to members of the royal family and their supporters, or to favourites of the king. Henry VII, however, did not do that; for example, the lands formerly held by Warwick 'the King-maker', Clarence and Gloucester were almost all retained in his own possession throughout his reign.

Second, although so many noble families failed to survive in the direct male line in Henry's reign, that does not mean that those which did survive gained extra land as a result, as had commonly happened in the past. In fact, in virtually every case the inheritances of extinct peerage families did *not* pass to other peers. Instead, their estates either went to the crown or were dispersed among co-heiresses who married members of the country gentry, not peers. It is impossible, at present, to explain this. It may simply have been the result of genetic accidents but, conversely, it is possible that Henry, who took a close interest in the marriages of his nobles, may himself have ensured in some cases that leading magnates and their sons did not marry heiresses. At any rate, there were no spectacular marriages uniting two or more substantial inheritances during the reign.

Third, some of the spectacular marriages made earlier, under Edward IV, by the family of Edward's queen Elizabeth Woodville, probably had a significant long-term effect. Admittedly, Elizabeth's elder son by her first marriage, Thomas Grey (created marquess of Dorset by his stepfather Edward IV), is one example of a magnate who held a combination of inheritances in Henry VII's reign: he had his paternal inheritance and a substantial share of the inheritances of both his wives, and he lived until 1501 and left a son to carry on his line. But that is outweighed by the fact that Elizabeth Woodville had six sisters, who all married magnates or sons of magnates (creaming off nearly all the most eligible bachelors of the period). Their husbands' families were prevented from gaining heiresses in that generation – which must have helped to restrict the accumulation of additional estates by surviving magnate families during the last quarter of the fifteenth century.

It would, of course, be wrong to state that there were no 'super-nobles' in Henry VII's reign: for example, in addition to Dorset, there were the heads of two ancient magnate families, the Stafford dukes of Buckingham and the Percy earls of Northumberland. Nevertheless, in Henry VII's reign no new families of 'super-nobles' appeared, either through royal favour or through fortunate marriages. Also, Dorset was kept under close royal control; Edward Stafford, third duke of Buckingham, was only seven years old in 1485 and did not enter his inheritance until 1498; and Henry Percy, fourth earl of Northumberland, died in a riot in 1489, leaving a ten-year-old son who did not come of age until 1499. Thus, partly through policy, partly through accidents, Henry VII did not have to contend with 'super-nobles' to anything like the same extent as previous English kings. This was especially the case during the 1490s, when Henry was engaged in the crucial task of consolidating his grip on the kingdom.

Over the reign as a whole, moreover, it is clear that the English nobility was not as impressive in numbers and (more importantly) in the extent of its possessions as under most of Henry's predecessors. The late medieval English nobility may not have killed itself off during the Wars of the Roses, but it had changed significantly by the end of the fifteenth century. And if its members were neither so numerous nor so powerful as in the past, then they were unlikely to have posed such a potential threat to the king.

Henry VII and the nobility

Did Henry VII actually see the leading nobles as a potential threat and set out to tame them? The traditional account of his reign argued that, but more recently historians have stressed that Henry was not consciously anti-noble. Many of his closest companions were nobles, like the earls of Oxford and Shrewsbury; he positively encouraged them to come to the royal court; forty-one were at least occasional attenders in the royal council; and they were employed on all kinds of tasks at the centre and in the localities. Also, it is emphasized nowadays just how much all the kings of this period had to depend on their nobilities. In the absence of a standing army, police force and extensive bureaucracy it was simply impossible for any government to keep a grip on the kingdom without the co-operation of the most powerful men in the state – and Henry VII was well aware of the fact.

Nevertheless, the crown's attitude to the nobility probably did change significantly in Henry's reign. For a start, favours and other forms of royal patronage were much more limited than in earlier reigns; and the difference between Henry's patronage and that of his predecessors was not simply a matter of scale. Edward IV and Richard III both tried (especially early in their reigns) to

16

buy loyalty through patronage. Under Henry VII, on the other hand, patronage had to be earned. Henry could reward good service generously – but the reward had to be deserved and would not be given in advance.

This stress on good service is reflected in *Fulgens and Lucres* (32), a play written in the 1490s by a lawyer in the household of Cardinal Morton, the archbishop of Canterbury. In it two suitors competed for a beautiful heiress: one was the head of an ancient magnate family, while the other had risen from humble origins through government office. The lady said she would marry whichever was the more noble, and the suitors' 'disputation' over this provides the play's climax. The first suitor based his claims on his hereditary status, whereas the second did so on the grounds of public service – and *he* won the lady. The play's message is clear: heredity is meaningless unless accompanied by virtuous actions; nobility is a matter of behaviour, not birth; high status and respect cannot be inherited but must be earned.

Fulgens and Lucres was presumably written for Cardinal Morton and probably – since Morton headed Henry VII's government – for the king as well. Certainly Henry would have agreed with the message. Its contemporary relevance is highlighted by the fact that Edmund Dudley, the Sussex lawyer who became one of Henry's right-hand men, 'used his title of king's councillor as proudly as any peerage' (9). To men like Dudley, prestige came from royal service, not hereditary titles. The audience of *Fulgens and Lucres*, indeed, would surely have envisaged a hereditary grandee like the duke of Buckingham as the unsuccessful suitor and a royal administrator like Edmund Dudley as the successful one. But *Fulgens and Lucres* is not hostile to all nobles – just those whose behaviour does not maintain what it declares to be the noble ideal of good service to the state. The nobles closest to Henry VII did fulfil that ideal: men such as Jasper Tudor; or the earl of Oxford, whose military role has already been stressed; or George Talbot, earl of Shrewsbury, another of the most conspicuous servants of the early Tudor monarchy; or Giles Lord Daubeney, one of the few men whom Henry promoted to the peerage.

17

Thomas Howard, earl of Surrey, was another noble who earned Henry's favour through good service. His father, John Lord Howard, was heir to the Mowbray dukes of Norfolk, received most of that inheritance, many other estates and the title duke of Norfolk from Richard III, and died leading Richard's vanguard at Bosworth. Thomas was also a prominent henchman of Richard III, who made him an earl. After Bosworth he was imprisoned, and both he and his late father were 'attainted', that is, they and all their descendants were prohibited from ever possessing or inheriting land. But gradually he recovered his high position. The first step came in 1487, while he was still in prison, for during the Lambert Simnel rebellion the lieutenant of the Tower offered to release him, but he refused to accept freedom except from Henry VII himself. This episode probably helped assure Henry of Thomas's loyalty: he was released in 1489, his attainder was reversed and he was restored to his title. Initially, however, he was only allowed to receive his wife's inheritance, plus any lands which came from ancestors other than his father. Then, later that year, having earned favour by dealing with rebels in Yorkshire, he was given the original Howard family estates, but not those acquired by his father. And three years later, after further reliable service, he at last received his father's share of the duchy of Norfolk. But Henry VII never let him have the broad estates which Richard III had given his father, or the ducal title. It was only in 1513, when he won his victory over the Scots at Flodden, that he became duke of Norfolk. Other cases of attainder were treated similarly; the attainders were eventually cancelled, but the estates were only gradually and partially restored. This was one way in which Henry tried to ensure loyal service.

More typical of Henry's policy towards the nobility, however, was his use of 'recognizances' and other forms of financial pressure: 'the stick' (or threat of it) rather than 'the carrot'. A recognizance was a written undertaking to pay a certain sum of money if particular conditions were not kept; it was like being bound over to keep the peace or providing bail nowadays. Professor J. R. Lander's analysis of the subject (10) shows that well over half the peerage had to give recognizances to Henry at one time or another: 23 peers gave more than one, 11 gave 5 or more, 2 gave 12 and the unfortunate Lord Mountjoy gave 23. In all, no fewer than 39 of the reign's 60 peerage families were placed under recognizances or something similar. Also, peers often stood surety for other nobles and gentlemen; the earl of Shrewsbury gave recognizances worth £467 for himself, and was a part-guarantor of six other recognizances for sums totalling over £5500.

Henry did not use recognizances to raise money; generally, the sums for which they were given were not actually paid. Instead, their purpose was to impose the threat of heavy financial penalty for any future misdemeanour. Nobles had to provide financial guarantees – and often had to get others to provide such guarantees, too – for their loyalty and good behaviour. The result, Professor Lander has concluded, was that towards the end of the reign there developed

> an immensely tangled, complicated series of relationships in which a majority of the peerage were legally and financially in the king's power. . . . The system was so extensive that it must have created an atmosphere of chronic watchfulness, suspicion, and fear.

The earl of Shrewsbury's recognizances show how a staunch supporter of the king could be caught up in the system. But he escaped mildly by comparison with Edward IV's stepson, Thomas Grey, marquess of Dorset. In 1483 Dorset had fled from Richard III's England to Henry Tudor, but subsequently Henry had had to prevent him forcibly from defecting back to Richard. After that Henry never trusted him and, indeed, temporarily imprisoned him during the Lambert Simnel rebellion of 1487. In 1492 he fell foul of the king again. This time he was required to transfer all his lands except two manors to trustees who would hold them for the king, give a recognizance for £1000, and find others who would give recognizances worth £10,000 on his behalf. Even when this agreement was cancelled, probably in 1496, Dorset was apparently required to provide securities to the value of £2800 for his good behaviour. Not surprisingly, after 1492 he gave Henry VII no further cause for concern.

Dorset was one of the 'super-nobles' who had survived from before 1485. Two others, the earl of Northumberland and the duke of Buckingham, were put under similar pressures. In 1504, for instance, the fifth earl of Northumberland had to give a recognizance for £2000, and in 1505 he was fined £10,000 for apparently abducting an heiress who was a royal ward. The fine was suspended, and instead the earl gave a £5000 recognizance and delivered some of his estates into the king's control, to be kept until half the fine had been paid off at the rate of £300 a year. Little was actually paid, because the agreement was cancelled after Henry VII's death; but Northumberland, like Dorset, was for a time under threat of utter financial ruin. The third duke of Buckingham, too, suffered from recognizances and fines. He was fined heavily because his mother married without royal licence in 1496, and because he entered into his own inheritance in 1498 before he was twenty-one. As usual the fines were not fully paid, but after Henry VII's death Buckingham stated that he had had to borrow money at great personal loss, had been wrongfully charged with debts and dues totalling over £7000, and had lost £3500 in legal expenses and revenues.

The examples of Dorset, Northumberland and Buckingham show that the greater the magnate, the more likely Henry was to put him under some kind of financial pressure. This is true, too, of the Stanleys. Henry stayed on good terms with his stepfather, the first earl of Derby, until the latter's death in 1504, and significantly increased Derby's possessions in north-west England. But Sir William Stanley's execution showed that the family had no guarantee of permanent royal favour. And after the first earl of Derby's death, several of the second earl's relatives incurred huge fines totalling over £250,000, while the second earl gave recognizances for more than £2000 and made over nine manors to the king's trustees to pay off a 'debt' of over £5000 at some £270 a year.

Now recognizances can be found under Richard III, Edward IV and earlier kings, but until 1485 they were only employed occasionally and haphazardly. For Henry, on the other hand, they were the basis of a technique for exerting control over the nobility through a system of suspended sentences requiring good behaviour, which could, in the most serious cases, threaten complete ruin for a magnate if he displeased the king. In this respect Henry VII can

once again be contrasted with Edward IV and his other predecessors.

Henry's use of recognizances clearly demonstrates that,
although he was not consciously anti-noble and indeed appreci-
ated the nobility's vital importance to the state, he was prepared
to be extremely hard on individual nobles whenever he considered
it necessary. The main characteristic of his relations with the
nobles, in fact, is his determination to ensure (through recognizances, fines and other pressures) that they upheld what he himself
considered to be the best interests of his kingdom. Henry VII's
nobility were expected to co-operate with the king, on the king's
own terms.

Retaining

Several of the fines and recognizances imposed by Henry VII were
for illegal retaining. Retaining – the recruiting by lords of gentry
followers – was very common in late medieval England. Lords
needed retainers to help look after their interests and affairs, and
the bigger the retinue the greater the lord's prestige. There was
nothing intrinsically wrong with that; if well organized and controlled, retinues could be a powerful force for stability. Moreover,
they were vital to the national war machine, making up the
greater part of every army of the period.

But there was another side to the coin. Retainers served their
lords in civil wars too. Indeed, retaining by magnates always
increased during periods of political tension, and retinues were
also extremely important in local quarrels. Nobles generally
pursued disputes by both fair means and foul – and the latter
normally involved the use of retinues as armed gangs, as numerous riots and skirmishes testify. Also, retinues enabled lords to
pervert the course of justice, by organizing biased juries, threaten-
ing unbiased ones, overaweing court proceedings and so on.
Moreover, this applied not only to nobles' disputes; a lord undertook to uphold his retainers' interests by 'good lordship', which
meant taking part in the quarrels of individual members of his
retinue. Retaining was one of the most serious problems of late
medieval England, because of such consequences.

Henry VII's reign saw several statutes and royal proclamations concerning retaining, including general condemnations and prohibitions in 1485, 1487 and 1504. Past historians saw these as one of the reign's main achievements: Henry's abolition of 'livery' (giving a retainer a uniform or badge) and 'maintenance' (perverting judicial proceedings on a retainer's behalf) was once a textbook commonplace. Later work, however, showed that the legislation was part of a long sequence, and largely repeated Edward IV's act of 1468 against retaining. Also, despite their legislation, neither Edward IV nor Henry VII actually abolished retaining. Both kings (and their successors) still relied heavily on nobles' retinues for their armies; and at times in the sixteenth century these retinues still disturbed the peace, just as in the fifteenth century. The conclusion nowadays, therefore, tends to be that neither Edward IV nor Henry VII had much real success in dealing with retaining.

That conclusion is probably valid for Edward IV. Although the 1468 statute prohibited all retaining except that of domestic servants, estate officials and legal advisers, there was a major loophole: it excluded retaining for 'lawful service done or to be done'. After 1468, lords simply stated that their retaining was for lawful purposes, and otherwise retained as before. Professor Ross, indeed, argues that the act was merely a public relations exercise agreed by Edward and his nobles following complaints about retaining in the House of Commons, and that it was never intended to be enforced (21). This is borne out by Chief Justice Hussey's statement to Henry VII in 1485 that although in 1468 the lords swore to keep Edward's statute, within an hour he saw them breaking it openly.

Now Henry VII's statutes also have exclusions. In 1487 it was enacted that the existing legislation (the 1468 act, with its loophole) was to be upheld, while the 1504 act did not apply to servants, officials and lawyers, and permitted those persons 'the which by the virtue of the king's placard or writing signed with his hand and sealed with his privy seal or signet' to recruit men in order 'to do the king's service in war or otherwise at his commandment'. Clearly, Henry VII never intended to do away with retaining altogether. On the other hand, the most recent analysis of the subject (11) makes it equally clear that Henry's intentions and achievements with respect to retaining were in fact significantly different from Edward IV's.

Henry started in the 1485 parliament by making the Lords and Commons swear that they would not retain illegally. Since such an oath had also been given in 1468, Justice Hussey's misgivings are understandable. But Henry interpreted 'lawful' retaining much more strictly, as retaining which *the king* considered lawful. Admittedly, during the reign indictments for retaining are much commoner than formal prosecutions and punishments. But that, it has been shown, is because Henry's policy was not to prohibit retaining completely, but to challenge lords who retained and then make them assure the king – often through recognizances – that their retinues would not disturb the peace. The practice of retaining could thus be supervised. This led, in 1504, to the introduction of the special 'plàcards', or licences to retain, which had to be obtained from the king in person and which required the whole retinue to be listed for royal approval.

Did Henry's policy work? Two lords who flouted it were certainly dealt with severely. Under the 1468 and the 1504 acts, the penalty for illegal retaining was £5 per month per retainer, and that was applied literally in 1506 when Lord Burgavenny and Sir James Stanley (uncle of the second earl of Derby) were fined no less than £70,550 and £245,610 respectively. Although the fines were suspended, heavy recognizances were imposed instead, and in both cases it seems that the illegal retaining was checked. These examples, however, are exceptional. More typical, probably, is the case of the earl of Devon, who gave a recognizance not to retain illegally in 1494, and then in 1506 had to pay part of the sum due, presumably because he had broken his promise. Even the earl of Oxford was indicted for retaining and, it was said later, suffered financially as a result.

Henry VII's policy generally involved informal action, so it is impossible to assess it quantitatively. But the retinues of individual magnates, such as the duke of Buckingham and the earl of Northumberland (29, 28), have been found to be significantly smaller than those of their predecessors in previous reigns and to be limited to servants, officials and lawyers. Admittedly the numbers of Buckingham's and Northumberland's estate officers increased considerably; that was probably used as a partial way round the retaining statutes. Nevertheless, the fact that this method did not appear until Henry VII's reign is significant. Similarly, 'the most immediate difference between Henry's reign and its predecessors is that to date no example of private retaining by indenture [that is, a written contract, common before 1485] has come to light' (11). Lords may have retained without royal permission under Henry VII, but they did not leave written records of the fact that they had done so. This is good evidence that nobles were very conscious of Henry VII's strictness about retaining. And from that we may probably conclude that while Henry may not have been absolutely successful in solving the problem of retaining, he did, in contrast to Edward IV, go a long way towards controlling and restricting the practice.

Government in the localities

The issue of retaining is part of the much wider subject of local government. Late medieval England was governed by what seemed in theory a sophisticated and efficient system, backed up by the highly developed common law. The local administrative and legal machines were run by a network of sheriffs, coroners, escheators, justices of the peace and other officials; they were all directed from the centre through constant streams of written commands (especially a multitude of standardized 'writs'), and were supervised by various judges and commissioners under the ultimate control of the king and his council. Unfortunately, in practice this system suffered from two fundamental problems. First, the machinery of government had become extremely cumbersome and slow. This was especially true of legal proceedings: it was easy to start lawsuits, but the law was so complex and the lawyers were so ingenious that it was virtually impossible to stop cases from dragging on for years and years. Second, the notion of impartial 'public service' usually carried little weight. All agents of government, from the kings downwards, had no scruples about putting their private interests first if these clashed with public ones. As a result, the formal machinery for governing

24

late medieval England's localities was all too often hopelessly bogged down and corrupted.

The localities were also run through informal mechanisms, headed by the great local nobles. When a region or shire was dominated by one particular magnate, it could be run effectively and peacefully. But in late medieval England regions and shires commonly contained the spheres of influence of two or more magnates, and such circumstances frequently led to disruptive rivalries and feuds. Feuding sometimes derived from the magnates' own quarrels, but also often grew out of disputes among the local gentry. Disputing gentry generally sought magnate support, and that was usually forthcoming (by fair means and foul, as we have seen), because otherwise the magnates risked losing 'face', prestige and ultimately local power. Local gentry, in fact, often apparently played off rival magnates against one another, and so sucked them and their retainers into relatively minor disputes. And, of course, when central government was weak or incompetent, aristocratic feuding became worse and worse; indeed, one very influential analysis explains the Wars of the Roses themselves largely in terms of the escalation of local feuds (18).

How could this situation be improved? Neither Edward IV nor Henry VII made great changes in the existing machinery of local government. Instead, they tried to make it work better, especially with respect to the landowning classes, in two main ways. One was through direct supervision: for example, by travelling round the country, by intervening in disputes, by placing members of the royal household in local offices and, when necessary, by making local troublemakers appear before the king and royal council. The second way was through the delegation of regional authority: by entrusting areas of the country to chosen individual magnates, who were powerful enough to outface any rivals, settle disputes and generally control the local government. Both methods can be found under both Edward IV and Henry VII – but the balance between them in each reign was very different.

Edward IV worked fairly energetically to deal with and supervise local affairs in person and through his council and household. But, more significantly, he divided the country into several great power-blocks, each under individual magnates who can be described as

25

'regional troubleshooters'. Only the southern midlands and south-east were outside this scheme; they were run directly by the king himself. Otherwise, by the end of Edward's reign, the territorial pattern was roughly as follows: in the north-east (including part of Yorkshire), the earl of Northumberland; in south Lancashire, Cheshire and north Wales, Thomas Lord Stanley and Sir William Stanley; in the rest of the north, Richard duke of Gloucester; in the northern midlands, William Lord Hastings, Edward's chamberlain and close companion; in the east midlands and East Anglia, John Lord Howard, acting for Edward's young second son; in Wales, the prince of Wales, under the effective control of his mother's brother, Anthony Woodville, Earl Rivers; and in the south-west, the queen's eldest son by her first marriage, Thomas Grey, marquess of Dorset. Within each power-block the 'regional troubleshooter' was made dominant by grants of land (if necessary), by appointments to royal offices, commissions of *oyer et terminer* (to 'hear and determine' and so deal with disputes and crimes) and commissions of the peace (enabling them to supervise the local JPs), and by being allowed to control the local operation of royal patronage. With the king's backing, he was expected to arbitrate in and settle local feuds, and thus restore stability to the localities.

It is difficult to say how effective this was. While there is much evidence of local lawlessness (largely due to the problem of retaining), the situation towards the end of the reign does not seem as bad as in the 1440s and 1450s. Moreover, magnate feuding does appear to have ceased – at least until Edward's death. But that indicates the policy's fatal flaw. Edward had given great, largely autonomous, local authority to a very small number of nobles. They were mostly close to him, but they were potentially 'overmighty' and, because of the internal tensions within the royal family, were potential rivals. Furthermore, although it was useful to establish one dominant noble in a region, the corollary is that other nobles who were left out of the power-block pattern had a vested interest in seeing it collapse. Edward's power structure was too narrowly based, and so was inherently unstable. Within a few months of his death it had disintegrated into a great *national* feud among most of the regional potentates.

After 1485, although Edward's system of local control had been destroyed, some of the regional potentates did survive: Lord Stanley (now earl of Derby), the fourth earl of Northumberland and the marquess of Dorset. Also, Jasper Tudor was restored to his Welsh estates and rewarded with extra land, and so was the earl of Oxford in East Anglia. Thus, even had he wanted to, Henry VII could not have done away with strong regional nobles altogether. The Stanleys, indeed, continued to control Lancashire and Cheshire; Oxford wielded great local influence in East Anglia; and (until 1495) Jasper Tudor was the main power in much of Wales. The marquess of Dorset, on the other hand, lost almost all his regional power. And in the north-east, where the earl of Northumberland's dominance had already been undermined by Richard III, Henry did little to help him re-establish himself. Northumberland had been imprisoned after Bosworth, and although he was soon released and reappointed to the Percies' accustomed position of warden on the borders with Scotland (one of the main sources of Percy power), the terms of his appointment were significantly restricted. In the later 1480s Northumberland seems desperate for royal favour – which Henry VII would not bestow. The indirect result was his death in 1489, when he tried, against his better judgement, to carry out the king's command and enforce tax-collection in Yorkshire. Anti-tax rioters killed him after he had been deserted by his retainers, who, through his lack of royal favour, had been deprived of 'good lordship'.

Northumberland's death left a power vacuum (his son was well under age) which Henry filled by entrusting local responsibility to Thomas Howard, earl of Surrey. That was not simply the replacement of one magnate by another, for Surrey had no land in the region; he was an outsider who owed his position purely to the king, from whom he was hoping to earn the restoration of his forfeited estates. Surrey looked after the north-east for Henry until 1501. He was then replaced, not by the fifth earl of Northumberland, but by a council in the north under the archbishop of York. This was not a complete innovation; Richard III had had a council for Yorkshire. But it was a significant step away from the idea of entrusting a region to a local potentate; the fifth earl of Northumberland, indeed, was not initially even appointed to the council.

Wales was treated similarly. There, Edward IV's eldest son, the prince of Wales, had had a council, but that had been largely under the control of Earl Rivers. Under Henry VII, Prince Arthur's council was similar (with extensive judicial and administrative powers), but after Jasper Tudor's death it was not dominated by any one magnate. And, when Arthur died, it continued in existence under the presidency of the bishop of Lincoln. Thus a council for Wales came to be established independently of the prince. The cases of Wales and the north-east demonstrate, therefore, that – unlike Edward IV – Henry VII was not content to entrust large regions of the country to local potentates. In general, indeed, he probably avoided that particular way of looking after the localities wherever possible. Certainly his reign saw no equivalent of Edward IV's power-block policy.

Instead, central supervision was the keynote of Henry's policy for the localities. Unlike Edward IV he did not travel extensively round the kingdom, but, from Westminster and his favourite palace at Richmond, he seems to have made the crown's authority widely and effectively felt. His methods were partly traditional. As under earlier kings, but probably to an even greater degree, members of his own household were appointed to local offices and wardenships of royal castles, especially in areas where they were already landowners. He continued the steady expansion in the tasks and responsibilities laid on the JPs (mostly members of the local gentry), and stimulated their efficiency both by formalizing and publicizing a complaints procedure against them, and by having household men and royal councillors included among their number. And third, like his predecessors, he encouraged victims of local lawlessness or corruption to seek redress through the royal council and its offshoots – but he expanded the conciliar mechanisms and increased their effectiveness.

More originally, Henry made use of his position as the kingdom's greatest landowner. Earlier kings, including Edward IV, had used the crown lands chiefly for patronage; many were given away and political control over the remainder had mostly gone to local magnates. Henry VII, in contrast, kept most of the crown lands (which had been greatly augmented by forfeitures) in his own possession, ran them through trusted officials like

Sir Reginald Bray, and exploited them not only for revenue (see pp. 43–5) but to extend his local authority. Thus in 1487 it was enacted that those who held lands, tenancies or offices from the crown could only be retained by the king. This deprived local nobles of many potential retainers and helped to give Henry substantial power bases in most shires. Henry also exploited the fact that, legally, the king was the superior feudal lord of every landowner, by sending out numerous commissions of enquiry to assert his feudal rights over the nobles (especially concerning the wardship and marriage of under-age heirs and heiresses), and to challenge their relationships with their own gentry tenants. Moreover, he recruited leading gentry to his own service; in the north-east, it has been shown, he 'poached' several who would otherwise have belonged to the earl of Northumberland's following (28), and that was probably also the case elsewhere. What all these points indicate is that, in most regions, Henry was trying to establish the crown as the chief local lord: the main focus for loyalty, the main source of patronage and, most importantly, the main figure to whom the local gentry should turn for help in settling their disputes. Instead of using 'regional troubleshooters' as Edward IV had done, Henry was making himself the 'trouble-shooter-in-chief' for almost every part of the kingdom.

But how did he tackle what was probably the main local government problem, the numerous gentry disputes? The standard modern accounts say his law and order record is unimpressive, because there is little evidence that he had serious cases prosecuted successfully either before the royal council or in the formal law courts. The evidence, however, has probably been misinterpreted. Cases before the royal council normally started when one of the parties sued the other, so the absence of crown prosecutions is not significant. And in the central criminal court, the King's Bench, where the crown did prosecute, it has now been shown (11) that while minor cases were dealt with by the slow, formal process, important ones – especially involving riots and illegal retaining – were usually settled *informally*. The court rolls state either 'case halted' or 'the above-named appeared and compounded with the king', and there is often evidence that a recognizance was given to the king or the Attorney General.

29

This was a quick way of dealing with local disturbances. In March 1490 Leo Percy of Flixborough was indicted before the Lincolnshire JPs for taking 200 henchmen and riotously expelling Robert Sheffield from 20 acres of land on 3 February 1490. The case came before the King's Bench in the autumn, and was settled the following spring. 'In other words the whole business from riot to termination took just over a year, quite astounding speed by fifteenth-century standards' (11). But there was no formal punishment; instead, both Percy and Sheffield gave recognizances for future good behaviour, until it was decided who was the rightful owner of the disputed land.

Another illuminating case (13) is that of Margaret Kebell, a wealthy widow and heiress. In February 1502 she was abducted by Roger Vernon – heir of Sir Henry Vernon of Haddon, a leading Derbyshire gentleman – and made to marry him. She subsequently escaped and accused the Vernons of illegal abduction, specifically prohibited by an act of 1487. Unfortunately the impossibility of finding unbiased juries in Derbyshire and the ingenuity of the defence lawyers meant the common law case dragged on inconclusively for years. But Margaret also went directly to Henry VII in person, and her suit against the Vernons was quickly heard by the royal council. Although here, too, clever defence prevented Margaret from actually winning, the Vernons eventually had to pay heavily to have the case dropped: Roger undertook to pay £266, Sir Henry to pay £900. It was a severe punishment; Edmund Dudley later believed that 'Sir Henry Vernon was too sore dealt with'.

Although the subject needs further research, these cases give a clear idea of Henry's policy. He apparently had little confidence that formal common law proceedings would produce the desired results and so preferred to settle disputes informally, as quickly as possible, by exerting royal pressure on the parties involved. His chief instrument was the recognizance. We have already seen how important this device was in his relations with the nobility, but many more recognizances were in fact exacted from the gentry. A quick survey of the *Calendars of Close Rolls* for the reign has yielded just over 700 entries concerning recognizances or similar bonds, of which almost 500 involved gentry. The majority of these were almost certainly intended to help maintain the peace. A fairly typical brief entry is: 'Recognizance to the king for £500 by Thomas Brandon knight. Condition: Thomas and his household servants to keep the peace against Robert Wylloughby lord Broke and his household servants' (May 1506). But many of the entries involve several gentlemen and, according to the editor of the *Calendars*, 'it is clear from the original recognizances surviving in unsorted Chancery Files that the great majority of them were not enrolled' on the Close Rolls. Clearly, therefore, many more than 500 gentlemen were involved. Indeed, it seems safe to conclude that during Henry VII's reign – especially during the later years, when recognizances are most common – *thousands* of country gentlemen must have been bound under recognizance to the king. This, admittedly, may not have completely solved the problems of fifteenth-century local government. But it is good testimony to much more direct royal control than in the past, which almost certainly resulted in a higher degree of local stability.

Central government

At the centre of all fifteenth-century government lay the royal council. It consisted of the king's councillors, or chief advisers – in other words, the king's right-hand men. Its function was to advise the king and help him carry out all his tasks of government; because of that the council obviously had an all-embracing competence. Its only limitation, indeed, was the limitation on the king's personal power: it could not sentence people to death or forfeiture, or make permanent decisions in lawsuits over land-ownership, for those things could only be done by 'due process of law' in the common law courts.

In Henry VII's reign the council and councillors were extremely prominent – so much so that it used to be thought that he originated the famous Tudor Star Chamber court based on the council, and that that was the basis for his strong government. This assumption derived from a statute of 1487 entitled 'for the Star Chamber', which established a tribunal consisting of certain royal councillors with powers to deal with lawlessness. But, as historians have now been stating for many years, the title is a later, mistaken addition: the statute did not mention the words 'Star Chamber', and it had nothing to do with the later court. Admittedly there was a 'Star Chamber' in Henry's reign; it was not a court, however, but a room at Westminster with stars painted on the ceiling in which the royal council commonly met when it was considering judicial matters – as it had been accustomed to do throughout the fifteenth century. Furthermore, it is pointed out that in practice the royal council under Henry VII acted much as it had always done. Nor was there much new about the councillors: the employment of 'new men' in Henry's central government is another traditional idea that has been discredited. Thirty of Henry's councillors were councillors to one or other of the Yorkist kings, fifteen more were close relatives of Edward IV's councillors and several others had been Yorkist administrators. Also, the general structure of membership is the same under Henry as under his predecessors. A large number of men were sworn as councillors (the names of 227 are known for Henry's reign), but there were no more than two dozen regular attenders: the Chancellor, Treasurer, Keeper of the Privy Seal, a few bishops, one or two magnates, and some lesser peers, knights and lawyers. Indeed, the number of attenders most commonly recorded was only seven. This pattern of an inner core of regular councillors within a much larger body is common throughout the later middle ages.

Nevertheless, there were some major developments in the council's history under Henry VII, notably in the appearance of offshoots from the main council. Thus, while the title 'Star Chamber Act' is a mistake, the 1487 statute has recently been shown to be very important (14). The tribunal it established – consisting of the Chancellor, the Treasurer, the Keeper of the Privy Seal, two Chief Justices and two other royal councillors – did provide a supreme court to deal with riots, illegal retaining, perversion of justice and similar causes of local disorder. It was to conduct cases as it saw fit, and punish offenders 'in like manner and form as they should and ought to be punished if they were thereof convict after the due order of the law'. Therefore this tribunal had parliamentary authority to act as a common law court – but without the disadvantage of complex, technical and

32

slow procedures. This avoided the main contemporary problem about combating disorder: that common law proceedings were inconclusive and open to manipulation, and that the king and council, while able to act much more quickly and directly, could not impose the most severe punishments. The 1487 tribunal *could* act quickly and *could* punish severely.

In view of this, it might seem surprising that only ten cases involving it are known (though more may have been lost). But probably its value to Henry VII was as a deterrent. Normally, the king and council dealt with serious local disorders by requiring recognizances from the parties involved. After 1487, if one of the parties refused to give the recognizance, or subsequently broke the peace, he could have expected to be summoned before the 1487 tribunal, to be found guilty by the king's chief councillors and to be subjected to a full, common law, punishment. The threat of such a procedure was probably one of Henry's major weapons in his attempts to uphold good government throughout the kingdom and it is significant that the tribunal was temporarily abolished in the reaction which followed Henry VII's death.

Other offshoots of the royal council which emerged during the reign included the council, or court, of audit, in which leading councillors together with the king audited the accounts for crown lands and other revenue sources; the council of requests, which offered remedies in 'poor men's causes'; and, most significantly, 'the council learned in the law'. The latter had come into existence by 1495. It possibly started as a council representing the king as landlord, for it was presided over by the chancellor of the duchy of Lancaster, the largest single unit of crown lands, and met in the duchy chamber at Westminster. But its competence soon included all aspects of the crown's territorial and feudal rights with respect to every landowner, not just the king's own estates. It initiated the enquiries into landowners' wardships, marriages and subtenancies (see p. 29); it collected the dues which landowners owed to the king; and, having developed into the royal 'debt-collecting agency', it also supervised the agreements made in bonds and recognizances. That, of course, brought it into the law enforcement process. In the latter years of the reign, indeed, the 'council learned' had become the most powerful of all Henry's central institutions of government (9) – and also the most hated, as is amply demonstrated by the reaction after Henry died, when its most zealous members Edmund Dudley and Sir Richard Empson were executed.

Another trend evident within Henry VII's council is the departmentalization of the great administrative offices of Chancellor (together with his deputy, the Master of the Rolls, in charge of the government's routine paperwork), the Keeper of the Privy Seal and the Treasurer. Under Edward IV, leading councillors moved in and out of these offices quite frequently (he had nine Treasurers), and were prominent in the council because of their relationship with the king rather than because of their offices. But, under Henry VII, offices were not exchanged in that way. When Cardinal Morton, the Chancellor, died in 1500, the Keeper of the Privy Seal, Bishop Fox of Exeter, did not move into the chancellorship (as might have happened earlier), but remained in his own office until 1516. Similarly, there were only two Treasurers between 1485 and 1522. This departmentalization not only affected the chief administrative posts; under them, 'there appeared a new layer of top civil servants' who could aspire to rise through a fairly clear career structure to one of the great government offices and, through that, *ex officio*, to become one of the king's chief councillors (14).

This brings us to the subject of personnel. For Henry VII's reign, as for Edward IV's, the full list of councillors divides fairly equally into nobles, courtiers, churchmen and officials and, as has been said, there was considerable continuity in the actual individuals. But among Henry VII's important, regular councillors there was a growing preponderance of lawyers, which is not found earlier. Thus the key 'council learned in the law' was staffed almost exclusively by common lawyers, while the top administrative offices (except the treasurership) and their subordinate secretariats became the preserve of men trained in 'civil' law (or 'Roman' law, a system which exalted the authority of the ruler far more than the common law did). And among the councillors who contemporaries reckoned had most influence with Henry – Cardinal Morton, Bishop Fox, Lord Daubeney, Sir Reginald Bray, Sir Thomas Lovell and Edmund Dudley – all except the soldier Daubeney had legal expertise of one sort or another.

Previous royal councils had had legal experts, of course, but Henry's was eventually dominated by them (9). That was something new – and perhaps gives slightly more weight to the traditional view of his 'new men' than the current orthodoxy would allow.

Now Morton, Fox and Daubeney, together with several other councillors such as Sir Richard Empson, Sir John Risley and the two Treasurers, Lord Dinham and the earl of Surrey, had already served one or both of the Yorkist kings in some capacity. Thus it could be argued that for all the contrasts between Edward IV's and Henry VII's attitudes to government, Henry's chief councillors were simply putting into effect what they and their colleagues had experienced before 1485. What seems to be more likely, however, is that experience had taught men like Morton about the flaws in the way that Edward IV governed England – such as the over-generous patronage, the tolerance of retaining, the delegation of too much independent authority to a small body of regional potentates, and the ignoring of dangerous rivalries within the royal family – and so they urged Henry VII to rule differently. We have seen Justice Hussey's cynicism about the value of demanding oaths not to retain illegally from the nobles, which derived from what had happened under Edward IV; other of Henry's councillors no doubt said much the same. Or consider the anonymous chronicler from Crowland Abbey who wrote of the events of 1483–5; as an ecclesiastical lawyer who worked in the royal chancery and sat in the royal council under Edward IV, he was from the same milieu as Morton, Fox and many other of Henry's councillors, and may himself have been one of them. What his chronicle shows is that 'he could perceive of the Yorkist age as a historical period after which there were new political realities calling for new policies. His recipe was for a cold, calculating government which distrusts its people and rules by eternal suspicion and vigilance' (14). That recipe was certainly followed under Henry VII! In other words, the continuity in personnel between Edward IV's and Henry VII's governments may well help to explain many of the differences between the two reigns.

Yet although they may have influenced him in the first year or so of his reign, it would be too much to suggest that Henry's policies were determined by his councillors rather than by himself.

It is, in fact, abundantly clear, as his main biographer Professor S. B. Chrimes has written, that 'the ultimate decision in matters about which he wished to decide for himself remained with him. There is no hint that the council or any of the councillors would, or could, overbear him. Henry was master in his own house' (5). His handwritten initials survive on numerous warrants directing all aspects of his government, and on every page (at one period after every entry) of his financial accounts. He annotated indictments, intervened in lawsuits and controlled royal patronage. Even his close councillors felt the effects. When Empson on one occasion was given a stewardship over some crown lands, a note in Henry's own handwriting changed it from a life grant to a grant during royal pleasure.

Probably the best contemporary testimony to Henry's personal rule comes from the petition written by Edmund Dudley while he was awaiting execution in 1510 (12). Dudley had been one of the executors of Henry's will, which had requested 'that restitution should be made to all persons by his grace wronged contrary to the order of his laws'; therefore, to bring 'help and relief for the dead king's soul', he went through his records and found eighty-four cases where he believed restitution ought to be made as Henry had wished. Among the list are several entries clearly demonstrating Henry's own responsibility; for example: 'Item the king's grace dealt hardly with young Clifton in his bond contrary to my will'; 'Item the king's grace dealt sore in the matter of my Lady Strange for her lands'; 'Item the Earl of Northumberland was bound to the king in many great sums, howbeit the king's mind was to have payment of £2000 and of no more, as his grace showed me, yet that was too much for ought that was known'. And in general, as Dudley also wrote, 'The king's grace . . . was much set to have many persons in his danger at his pleasure.' This kind of royal control by the king of the kingdom's affairs is the most striking aspect of central government during Henry VII's reign.

Foreign affairs

During the middle ages most people simply had one basic – if vital – requirement of their governments: to ensure that they could

live their lives in peace, with the minimum of trouble and inter-
ference. Thus the maintenance of security and stability was the
fundamental duty of any government. Now since, in Henry VII's
England, the main actual and potential threats to stability were
internal ones, posed by the landowning classes, much of this
pamphlet has concentrated on the crown's relations with the
nobility and gentry. But threats to stability could come from outside the kingdom as well as from within. In other words, defence
and the conduct of foreign affairs were as much a part of a crown's
obligation to its people as the maintenance of law and order. It is
now time, therefore, to turn to England's foreign affairs under
Henry VII.

At one level this is an extremely complicated subject. The late
fifteenth and early sixteenth centuries were the time of 'Renaissance diplomacy', when international relations stretched more
widely and changed more quickly than at any time in the past. A
full account would require discussion of Henry's dealings with
most major European states and many of the minor ones –
something which there is obviously no space to attempt here.
Instead, all that can be done is to stand back from the complexities
of day-to-day diplomacy and sketch what appears to be the broad
pattern of England's foreign affairs in the period. And, as we shall
see, at this more general level the picture is much simpler.

For most of the two centuries before 1485, England's foreign
affairs seem to have been conducted on the principle that attack
was the best form of defence. Although the national armies and
the taxes that paid them were both ostensibly raised for the
defence of the realm, they were in fact almost invariably used to
attempt foreign conquests in Scotland and France – especially
during the long conflict with France generally known as the
Hundred Years War (1337–1453). By the beginning of Henry
VII's reign, however, the Hundred Years War had at last come to
an end, with the final expulsion of the English from all their
conquests in France except Calais. Meanwhile the main focus of
international affairs had shifted to the Franco-Spanish wars, which
had broken out in Italy and did not directly concern England.
England was now on the sidelines of international politics, no
longer engaged in foreign conquests and not directly threatened

37

from abroad. For the old historians of Henry VII, this change in England's international situation was another 'new' aspect of the reign.

It has subsequently been pointed out, however, that the English expulsion from France took place long before the beginning of Henry VII's reign: Normandy was lost in 1450, Gascony in 1453. This means that Edward IV, not Henry VII, was the first English king to be free of the entanglement in France. Furthermore, despite that, both Edward IV and Henry VII maintained a token claim to the French throne (which English kings did not actually renounce until 1801). More significantly, they both led invasions of France, in 1475 and 1492, which were very similar; neither invasion achieved any military success, and both Edward IV and Henry VII were bought off with annual pensions of 50,000 gold crowns (£10,000) by the treaties of Picquigny (1475) and Etaples (1492) respectively. Relations with England's northern neighbour, Scotland, were also much the same in the two reigns: mostly peaceful, but with brief outbreaks of open hostilities. And, in general, both kings had to pursue similarly convoluted foreign policies in the extremely fluid world of Renaissance diplomacy. For these reasons, therefore, foreign affairs are another field in which the standard modern accounts tend to stress continuity from Edward IV to Henry VII.

Yet while the tortuous international situation of later fifteenth-century Europe meant that under both kings England's foreign relations were equally complicated, Professor Ross's detailed analysis of Edward IV's foreign policy (21) has now demonstrated that the similarities between it and Henry VII's are only superficial. For a start, Edward's European concerns concentrated on England's closest continental neighbours: France, Brittany, Burgundy (which included the Low Countries) and the North German Hanseatic League. Henry was also much concerned with these, but his diplomacy ranged further afield, as we can see from the treaties he made with Aragon and Castile in 1489 and 1496; from England's entry in 1496 to the 'Holy League' which the papacy, Austria, Aragon, Castile, Milan and Venice had all constructed against France; and from the marriage alliance he made with the Spanish kingdoms when his eldest son Arthur married Katherine, daughter of Ferdinand of Aragon and Isabella of Castile. This all reflects the transformation in the European diplomatic scene brought about by the outbreak of the Franco-Spanish conflict in Italy in 1494.

Moreover, Edward was much more aggressive towards France, wanting revenge on Louis XI for aiding his enemies in 1470–1; Henry VII, who had enjoyed French help in 1485, was more cautious and pragmatic. And the motives for their respective invasions were very different. In the three years before Edward invaded he made extensive diplomatic preparations, amassed considerable funds (some £160,000) through direct taxation and benevolences, and raised well over 11,000 troops who, when they set sail in July 1475, constituted the largest army sent to France thus far in the fifteenth century. Professor Ross's conclusion is that Edward was seriously hoping to regain some or all of the former English possessions in France. But – as the king knew – one essential prerequisite for English success in France was the active assistance of Louis XI's other enemy, the extremely powerful duke of Burgundy (who had married Edward's sister in 1468). In July 1475 the duke failed to honour his undertakings to Edward; this made the king's plans collapse, leaving him with no option but to extricate himself from France on the best terms possible.

Henry VII did not have such grandiose ambitions. His 1492 invasion simply originated in a commitment, which he had undertaken reluctantly in the treaty of Redon (1489), to help prevent the duchy of Brittany from being taken over by the French king. He did, admittedly, raise a slightly larger force than Edward IV (about 12,000 men (15), *not* the 26,000 given in some accounts), but apparently he spent rather less money on it, and the main point is that the invasion was not launched until October, far too late in the year to be a serious attack on France. In fact, Henry only campaigned for a week and then started negotiations, giving the inclement weather and the lateness of the season as his reasons for doing so. It is very difficult, therefore, to see the 1492 invasion as anything more than a powerful demonstration, designed to fulfil Henry's obligations to his allies and at the same time to force from the French the same kind of profitable settlement as Edward IV had gained – but without Edward's original aim of conquest.

Much the same can be said of the two kings' dealings with Scotland. They both concluded long truces, but it seems that Edward IV's (1474) was simply meant to keep Scotland quiet while he invaded France, whereas Henry VII's (1502) was intended to produce lasting Anglo-Scottish peace. During Edward's reign, the 1474 truce was broken by both sides, but a recent study of this from the Scottish point of view tallies with Professor Ross's conclusion that the escalation of border friction into open war in 1480-3 should be blamed chiefly on Edward IV, not on the Scots. He revived the old English claims to overlordship over Scotland in 1480 and launched an expensive invasion by 20,000 troops in 1482, which recaptured Berwick (gained by the Scots in 1461, the first year of Edward's reign) but failed in its other purpose of replacing the Scottish king with his rebel brother, who had agreed, in effect, to be an English puppet. A contemporary record of the king's anger at this failure proves that, towards the end of his reign, Edward was being as aggressive and unrealistic in his policy towards Scotland as he had been towards France.

Henry VII, in contrast, never threatened Scotland; the Anglo-Scottish warfare of 1496-7 was initiated by James IV, who supported the Perkin Warbeck conspiracy in the hope of recovering Berwick. Once English forces had checked the Scots invasion, Henry's diplomats quickly induced James to cease hostilities and (most significantly from Henry's point of view) abandon the Scottish support for Perkin Warbeck. The warfare of 1496-7 was, in fact, an aberrant interlude. The 'treaty of perpetual peace' of 1502 and its sequel the following year when James IV married Henry's daughter Margaret Tudor – 'the Marriage of the Thistle and the Rose' – is much more typical of the relations between the old enemies during Henry VII's reign.

Henry's diplomacy was thus more concerned with peace than with war. Its main aim, indeed, may well have been to help him maintain *internal* security. His own experience before and in 1485 would have made him only too well aware of the importance of foreign support for anyone who hoped to gain the throne. Not surprisingly, therefore, one constant feature of all his negotiations was the effort to secure undertakings from foreign rulers that they would not support Yorkist pretenders. The marriages of his children, too, not only strengthened diplomatic links but also helped to commit the rulers of the Spanish kingdoms and Scotland to maintaining the Tudor dynasty rather than its enemies. A neat, if tragic, illustration of the connection between dynastic marriages and internal security is given by the fact that, when negotiations for Arthur's marriage to Katherine of Aragon started in 1498, the Spanish ambassador indicated that Katherine's parents would be happier if not 'a drop of doubtful royal blood' was left in England (4). He meant the earl of Warwick, and this may help to explain Warwick's execution shortly afterwards.

Parliament and finance

The fact that neither Henry VII nor Edward IV waged long wars abroad had a profound influence on the parliamentary and financial history of the period. Parliament is one area where a contrast cannot be drawn between the two reigns: it is hard to disagree that Edward IV's is 'one of the least constructive and inspiring phases in the history of the English parliament', and that Henry VII's 'is one of the dimmer periods of parliamentary history' (21, 4). Indeed, although parliaments were the country's supreme legislative, judicial and fiscal institutions, they met remarkably infrequently at this time. In 23 years Edward IV summoned 6 parliaments which sat for 84 weeks in all, while in 24 years Henry VII summoned 7, which sat for 72 weeks; moreover, there were only 2, sitting for 17 weeks, in the years from 1497 to 1509.

This infrequency was due to several factors. Although both kings did, of course, use parliament for legislative purposes (and indeed the modern procedure of introducing government bills for readings in the Lords and Commons largely developed in this period), neither Henry nor Edward saw the need to initiate a large body of legislation; their commonest acts were acts of attainder against political enemies. Parliament's main judicial function as the final court of appeal had by this time been largely taken over (in practice if not in theory) by various judicial offshoots of the royal council. Also, the customs on wool and cloth exports had been granted for life to Edward IV in 1465 and to Henry VII in

1485, so these could be levied without regular parliamentary approval, as had been necessary earlier. And, most significantly, neither king had to ask for war taxation nearly as frequently as in the time of the Hundred Years War.

Nevertheless, this does not mean that parliament was no longer a vitally important part of England's political institutions. It was, in fact, firmly established as the forum in which the most important business affecting the kingdom as a whole had to be transacted. For example, the ratifications of Edward IV's, Richard III's and Henry VII's seizures of the throne were all enacted in parliaments; so was the legislation against disorders, riots and retaining, which legitimized Henry VII's dealings with individual nobles and gentry; and so was the statute giving the 1487 tribunal power to impose common law punishments. In the 1504 parliament, moreover, there was a fairly traditional clash over taxation – in which Henry had to compromise following opposition in the Commons. So although parliaments took place infrequently in this period, there was no danger that they would have ceased to meet altogether; circumstances necessitating their meeting always occurred sooner or later.

At first sight the fiscal history of the two reigns is equally similar. Edward IV's predecessor, Henry VI, had been the most insolvent of all medieval English kings, but Edward IV and Henry VII both managed to keep the crown's finances solvent. The main reason for this is that neither had to spend very much on warfare. Direct taxation of the laity took place in only five years under Edward IV, and in only seven years under Henry VII. There was also little difference between the two kings' other sources of revenue: taxation of the clergy was somewhat more regular than lay taxation in both reigns; they both had the customs on exports; they both occasionally exploited 'forced loans' and 'benevolences' (when wealthy subjects were asked to make gracious loans or gifts to the king, which were extremely hard to refuse); and after 1475 and 1492, respectively, both enjoyed an annual £10,000 subsidy from France.

In addition, the crown lands made a much greater contribution to the royal finances in these two reigns than under previous fifteenth-century kings, especially Henry VI. This was due partly to the effects of inheritances and forfeitures in the period, but also to the system of 'chamber finance', an innovation of Edward IV's. In place of the slow, bureaucratic and very wasteful system of managing the crown lands which the medieval exchequer had operated, Edward IV introduced a simpler, more flexible and much more lucrative system in which revenues were sent by collectors ('receivers') directly to his own private financial office, the royal 'chamber'. After Bosworth, the exchequer officials reintroduced the old methods, but within a few years Henry VII, too, was using the system of chamber finance with great success. Here, then, is another aspect of continuity between the two reigns; indeed, the account of the administration of the crown lands in this period (16) is a vital plank in the modern 'continuity thesis'.

But how much money did the two kings actually have? The question can only be answered roughly, since a detailed analysis would be too complex for this pamphlet and, anyway, absolutely precise figures cannot be given. Nevertheless, it is clear that Henry VII's revenues were substantially higher than Edward IV's. The total which Henry raised from direct taxation of the laity, for instance, came to some £280,000, whereas Edward only received about £180,000. The yields from clerical taxation were closer, but the total for Henry VII is still slightly higher – probably some £160,000 as opposed to £130,000. The yield from the customs went from an average of about £25,000 in the first half of Edward's reign to around £34,000 in the second half; under Henry VII it stayed at nearly £34,000 between 1485 and 1495, and then rose to some £40,000 on average. Edward's benevolence of 1474–5 raised about £25,000; Henry's of 1491 is said to have produced over £48,000. Edward had the £10,000 French pension for only seven years, from 1475 to 1482 (when it was cancelled); Henry enjoyed it for the sixteen years from 1492 to the end of his reign. As for the crown lands, in Edward's last years it has been estimated that they were producing about £10,000 a year, and possibly 'much less' (21); in Henry VII's last years, on the other hand, the annual revenue from the crown lands has been calculated at some £42,000. The result was that in his later years Edward IV had a regular income of roughly £60–65,000 a year, whereas the comparable figure for the final stages of

Henry VII's reign was probably comfortably over £100,000. (In both cases the totals are made up of the revenues from the customs, the crown lands, the French pension and £5–10,000 of miscellaneous income.)

The most striking difference is clearly in the yield of the crown lands, and these also require fuller consideration because of the importance attached to Edward IV's system of chamber finance. The main point about them, in fact, is not how they were administered, but that they produced far more for Henry VII than for Edward IV. This is due partly to increased administrative efficiency; Henry audited his chamber accounts meticulously, driving his receivers much harder than Edward had done to produce the maximum revenue. But, as Professor Ross has stressed, the main reason is that Edward IV, unlike Henry VII, actually granted a very high proportion of the crown lands away, especially to his family (21).

At the beginning of Edward's reign the basic royal estates, his personal inheritance and the lands of forfeited enemies meant that the crown lands covered the principality of Wales and the territories of six dukes, six earls, seven other peers and dozens of wealthy gentlemen – far more than at any time since the Norman Conquest of 1066. But most of these lands were quickly dispersed to Edward's brothers the dukes of Clarence and Gloucester, to the earl of Warwick and the rest of the Nevilles, and to his Woodville relatives and to other nobles, while Wales, Cornwall and Chester went to his eldest son in 1472. The fresh acquisitions made in 1471 were also soon granted away, and so was part of the Clarence estate, confiscated in 1478. Thus, because of Edward IV's generosity, the crown lands did not provide him with nearly as much revenue as they might have done.

Henry VII treated his territorial acquisitions very differently. In 1485 he took over Richard III's royal and personal territories plus several estates forfeited by Richard's supporters, and during his reign he received a considerable number of windfalls from forfeitures, escheats (when landowners died without heirs) and wardships. That gave him territorial gains which were roughly comparable with Edward IV's – but *he* kept most of them in his own possession. In the last years of his reign, his crown lands included the principality of Wales; the duchies of Cornwall, Lancaster and York; the earldoms of Chester, March, Pembroke, Richmond, Salisbury, Suffolk and Warwick; the estates of several lesser peers and wealthy gentry; and various wardships which on their own yielded over £6000 a year. Now part of the reason for this, of course, is that Henry only had a small number of close relatives to provide for, and several of these died during his reign (Jasper Tudor in 1495, Prince Arthur in 1502, Queen Elizabeth in 1503). Yet there is more to the point than that. As has already been indicated, Henry VII was far less generous with grants of land to his family and to other nobles than Edward IV had been. His retention of the revenues from his second son's estates is a particularly striking illustration of this (see pp. 10–11).

Thus Henry VII's attitude to the crown's territorial possessions contrasts sharply with Edward IV's. Although he did not see them exclusively as a source of money, it does seem that – particularly in his later years – revenue took priority over other considerations. With Edward IV, by contrast, the other consider-ations (especially commitments to his family and supporters) were more important than the need for revenue in determining what he did with the crown lands. The result was that Henry's income was significantly higher than Edward's, enabling him not just to get by financially but to do so comfortably and, at the same time, leave a substantial surplus – jewels and plate worth some £300,000 – at the end of his reign. This difference between the two kings greatly outweighs the similarity in the methods they used to administer their lands.

Henry's policy, however, was not to amass money simply for the sake of it. Although he left an unpleasant reputation for extreme avarice, this probably derives from a misunderstanding of his policies. 'The kings my predecessors, weakening their treasure, have made themselves servants to their subjects' he told one of his councillors (8). As that implies, Henry equated money with political power. It was in order to strengthen the crown politically that he was so concerned with maximizing his regular income. And, conversely, it was to weaken potential rivals and trouble-makers that he put them under financial pressure. Although fines, recognizances and the like brought in over £30,000 in cash between

1504 and 1508, their primary purpose was not to raise money but to maintain a form of political discipline over the nobility and gentry. His treatment of the crown lands and his treatment of the landowning classes had the same ultimate end: to maintain his grip on the crown for himself and his dynasty.

Conclusion: revolution in government?

The argument of this pamphlet has been that the idea of continuity between Henry VII and his predecessors, especially Edward IV, is exaggerated; the contrasts between Henry VII's reign and Edward IV's are more important than the continuities. Now, in conclusion, a brief attempt will be made to suggest how these contrasts fit into the long-term context of English history.

The main point, of course, is that the significance of Henry VII's restoration of political stability extends far beyond the later fifteenth century. The vulnerability of the English crown goes back, in fact, to the early fourteenth century. Every reign from Edward II's (1307–27) to Henry VII's either began or ended with a royal deposition (except the brief reign of Henry V, 1413–22). Also, in the fourteenth and earlier fifteenth centuries, rebellions and political disturbances were almost as common as between 1450 and 1485. After 1485, in contrast, no English monarch lost his throne until Charles I in 1649; and while rebellions and political disturbances did not cease altogether, we can see with hindsight that, until the 'Great Rebellion' of 1641, they did not threaten the crown nearly as seriously as before Henry VII's reign.

Much the same kind of long-term contrast can be seen in other areas. For example, the problem of junior members of the royal family was a recurring, vitally important theme of English medieval history from the Norman Conquest until the death of Edward IV; but after 1485 royal families were much smaller (no junior branch was established until the reign of George III) and whenever the royal family became a major political issue, as under Henry VIII, the problem was not that there were too many close relatives of the monarch but too few. In foreign affairs, too, Edward IV's aggression towards France and especially Scotland echoes that of his predecessors from the late thirteenth century, whereas Henry VII's more pragmatic and pacific approach foreshadows the main direction of foreign policy under his sixteenth- and seventeenth-century successors (except for parts of Henry VIII's reign). Moreover, of course, the Anglo-Scottish marriage of 1503 paved the way for the eventual political union of the British Isles.

Similarly, the existence of great local magnates was much more of a long-term feature of English history before 1485 than afterwards. There were powerful nobles under Henry's successors, but none to compare with the 'super-nobles' of the fifteenth, fourteenth and, indeed, thirteenth centuries. Edward IV's replacement of forfeited enemies with new magnates, especially from his own family, is characteristic of most of his predecessors since 1066; so is his primary use of the crown's lands and resources for the purpose of patronage; so is his inability (and perhaps unwillingness) to tackle the problems of large and unruly retinues and the perversion of justice. And in his attempts to maintain local order by delegating responsibility to men whom he created regional potentates, he seems virtually to be reverting to the practices of the 'classic' feudal era of medieval Europe. As far as his approach to the fundamental problems of governing England is concerned, Edward IV can be described as a typical medieval monarch.

Now since personal rule was another of the hallmarks of medieval kingship, that might be said of Henry VII, too. However, the level and extent of Henry's personal control was much greater than that of any of his predecessors; indeed, in this respect he is perhaps unique (the only parallel that comes to mind is Philip II of Spain). What is more significant, however, is that – both through fortunate circumstances and royal policy – Henry came closer to solving the problems of governing England than any of his predecessors had done. Moreover, broadly speaking, both the circumstances and the policy continued under his successors. Thus, although much has often been made of his son's execution of Empson and Dudley, and the cancellation of many recognizances after Henry VII's death, Henry VIII himself and his daughter Mary both made significant use of recognizances to enforce obedience. And the general policy of maintaining close supervisory links with the local gentry typifies the Tudor regime as a whole; so does the use of spies and informers; so does the use of conciliar courts; and so does the emphasis on the nobility's earning rewards from the crown rather than expecting them automatically. Furthermore while Henry VIII, unlike his father, was conspicuously generous with peerage titles, subsequently, to use Dr Penry Williams' metaphor about the later Tudor nobility, 'there were many clusters of stars, but there were fewer luminous planets than before and very few supernovae' (33); that was much the same situation as under Henry VII.

A passage from the general conclusion to Dr Williams' recent study of *The Tudor Regime* is also extremely relevant here. Having discussed Henry VII's legacy from Edward IV, he states that 'this inheritance does not go far to explain the success of the Tudors'.

> How then did they maintain a stable regime and impose their will, albeit incompletely, upon important areas of national life? They did not base their government, as Edward IV had done, upon an alliance with great magnate families. Nor, in my opinion, did their strength reside in the creation of a new bureaucratic machine. In spite of the innovations of Cromwell and the attentiveness of Burghley the institutions of government remained slender and inadequate. Important as the Privy Council, the Secretaryship, and the lawcourts might be, they were stunted and fragile by comparison with the machinery of a modern state. But Tudor government should not be judged in such terms. The official bureaucracy conducted only one part of the political process. The driving thrust came from *ad hoc* commissions and the manipulation of landowning influence in the regions, both of them harnessed to energetic rule at the centre. The strength of Tudor government lay in a skilful combination of the formal and the informal, the official and the personal. (33, pp. 462–3)

In this analysis, quite clearly, Henry VII's place belongs with his son and grandchildren, not with his Yorkist predecessors.

As those familiar with the reign of Henry VIII will be aware, however, this passage by Dr Williams challenges the argument of

Professor G. R. Elton that the administrative reforms initiated in the 1530s by Henry's Secretary, Thomas Cromwell, amounted to a 'Tudor revolution in government'. That is a justly famous thesis, which revolutionized the study of Tudor history, but here is obviously not the place to discuss it in any detail. Nevertheless it can hardly be ignored in an attempt to view Henry VII's reign in a long-term perspective.

One comment must be made immediately: the English Reformation, which plays a very prominent part in Professor Elton's argument, did produce a new, indeed revolutionary, situation for the country's government. Yet the constitutional machinery through which the Reformation was carried out dated back to the fourteenth century, while – more relevantly here – the means by which the crown's ecclesiastical policy was imposed on the population seem very reminiscent of the ways in which Henry VII imposed political stability a generation earlier. Other developments of the 1530s, too, are perhaps less revolutionary than has been argued. Thus the claim that Henry VII governed through his own person and household and so was 'medieval', whereas Thomas Cromwell introduced 'modern' bureaucratic government directed by the Privy Council, is at best a half truth. Recent research, for instance, shows a significant household involvement in government during and after the 1530s, as Professor Elton now appears to accept (34). Moreover, Henry VII's personal government, as we have seen, was very different from that of his predecessors; and although his financial system may have been based on the royal chamber (a branch of the household), it was audited and therefore directed by an offshoot of the council, under the king's own supervision. Some of those influential with Henry VII were household men, but others were not; the only feature they had in common was that they were all members of the royal council (9). Now, admittedly, in institutional terms Henry VII's council differed from the reformed Privy Council introduced by Cromwell; Henry's was a large amorphous body, whereas the new Privy Council had only a dozen or so members, all heads of government departments. But actually the contrast is much less sharp, because in practice it was unusual for as many as a dozen councillors to attend meetings of Henry's council, and the men who made up the core of regular attenders either headed departments of state or were closely identified with specific aspects of the kingdom's government. It is arguable, therefore, that Cromwell's reform of the royal council was less sweeping in practice than has been claimed. Moreover, his institutionalization of administrative and judicial offshoots of the council has clear antecedents under Henry VII. And, indeed, it has been pointed out that Cromwell himself was one of the most famous beneficiaries of the new 'civil service' career structure which had come into existence in Henry VII's reign (14).

Similar comments could be made about the other details of Professor Elton's argument. However, the main thing about the argument as a whole is that it concentrates largely on institutional history – which, it may be suggested, can be misleading. We have already seen that from the history of the crown lands under Edward IV and Henry VII: both kings administered them through the same institutions, but Henry VII's attitude to them was very different from Edward IV's, and as a result they yielded him far more revenue. The point is that – as Dr Williams indicated in the passage quoted above – successful government depends as much on the purpose and vigour with which it is executed as on its institutions. In this case, since the fundamental attitudes behind the Tudor regime can be traced back to Henry VII, his reign is probably at least as significant as the 1530s in the history of English government.

Moreover since, as was argued above, Henry VII's achievement depended largely on his own incessant personal direction of government, is it possible to suggest that his true successors were not the monarchs who followed him but their great ministers who, like Henry VII, kept close personal control on all the strands of government? Were not Cardinal Wolsey, Thomas Cromwell and Lord Burghley all in a sense 'Henry VII substitutes', continuing Henry's task of maintaining stability in England through broadly similar means? And whether or not that idea is acceptable, the debt which the Tudor regime owed to Henry VII is clear. The most important revolution in government of the period was surely the restoration of a high degree of peace and stability throughout most of the country, and its architect was King Henry VII. For this reason, his victory over Richard III in August 1485 deserves to be reestablished as a major turning-point in English history.

Further reading

Place of publication is London unless otherwise stated.

A. General surveys

1 J. A. F. Thomson, *The Transformation of Medieval England* (Longman, 1983).

2 J. R. Lander, *Government and Community: England 1450–1509* (Edward Arnold, 1980).
(These are at present the two most recent surveys of the period covered by this pamphlet.)

3 G. R. Elton, *England under the Tudors* (Methuen, 1955; revised edn, 1974) – rather older now, but still excellent; it is one of the most famous general surveys of English history ever written, and deservedly so.

B. Henry VII: king and government

4 R. L. Storey, *The Reign of Henry VII* (Blandford, 1968) – the most lively and readable single book on Henry.

5 S. B. Chrimes, *Henry VII* (Eyre Methuen, 1972) – fuller but less lively; good on institutional history.

6 S. B. Chrimes, 'The reign of Henry VII', chapter 4 in S. B. Chrimes *et al.* (eds), *Fifteenth-century England.* (Manchester, Manchester University Press, 1972) – usefully summarizes no. 5.

7 S. B. Chrimes, 'The reign of Henry VII: some recent contributions', *Welsh History Review,* vol. 10 (1980–1), pp. 320–33 – a survey of recent work (1972–80), to supplement no. 5's extensive bibliography.

8 R. Lockyer, *Henry VII* (Longman, 2nd edn, 1983) – briefer, but very useful, especially on the machinery of government and other topics that this pamphlet only touches on; also has a good short selection of documents.

9 M. M. Condon, 'Ruling elites in the reign of Henry VII', chapter 5 in C. Ross (ed.), *Patronage, Pedigree and Power* (Gloucester, Alan Sutton, 1979) – the best single modern analysis of the reign.

10 J. R. Lander, 'Bonds, coercion and fear: Henry VII and the peerage', chapter 11 of his *Crown and Nobility, 1450–1509* (Edward Arnold, 1976) – the main study of crown–noble relations.

11 A. Cameron, 'The giving of livery and retaining in Henry VII's

reign', *Renaissance and Modern Studies* (published by Nottingham University), vol. 18 (1974), pp. 17–35 – an excellent study, which has been relied on very heavily in this pamphlet.

12 C. J. Harrison, 'The petition of Edmund Dudley', *English Historical Review,* vol. 87 (1972), pp. 82–99.

13 E. W. Ives, '"Agaynst taking awaye of Women": . . . the Abduction Act of 1487', chapter II in E. W. Ives *et al.* (eds), *Wealth and Power in Tudor England* (Athlone Press, 1978).

14 N. Pronay, 'The chancellor, the chancery and the council at the end of the fifteenth century', chapter 7 in H. Hearder *et al.* (eds), *British Government and Administration* (Cardiff, Wales University Press, 1974).

15 J. R. Hooker, 'Notes on the organisation and supply of the Tudor military under Henry VII', *Huntingdon Library Quarterly,* vol. 23 (1959–60), pp. 19–31.

16 B. P. Wolffe, *The Crown Lands, 1461–1536* (George Allen & Unwin, 1970).

C. The fifteenth-century background

17 R. A. Griffiths, *The Reign of Henry VI* (Ernest Benn, 1981) – especially chapter 20 for fifteenth-century lawlessness.

18 R. L. Storey, *The End of the House of Lancaster* (Barrie & Rockliff, 1966) – particularly for aristocratic feuding.

19 C. Ross, *The Wars of the Roses* (Thames & Hudson, 1976).

20 A. Goodman, *The Wars of the Roses* (Routledge & Kegan Paul, 1981) – especially chapter 5 for Henry's campaigns.

21 C. Ross, *Edward IV* (Eyre Methuen, 1974) – the main authority for this reign.

22 C. Ross, 'The reign of Edward IV', chapter 3 of *Fifteenth-century England* (see no. 6) – an excellent summary of no. 21.

23 C. Ross, *Richard III* (Eyre Methuen, 1981) – finishing off the Yorkists.

24 D. A. L. Morgan, 'The king's affinity in the polity of Yorkist England', *Transactions of the Royal Historical Society,* 5th series, vol. 23 (1973), pp. 1–25.

D. The nobility and gentry

25 K. B. McFarlane, *The Nobility of Later Medieval England* (Oxford, Oxford University Press, 1973) – possibly the most influential book

ever written on late medieval England.

26 T. B. Pugh, 'The magnates, knights and gentry', chapter 5 of *Fifteenth-century England* (see no. 6).

27 M. A. Hicks, 'The career of the fourth earl of Northumberland, 1470–89', *Northern History*, vol. 14 (1978), pp. 78–107.

28 M. James, *A Tudor Magnate and the Tudor State: Henry Fifth Earl of Northumberland* (University of York, Borthwick Papers, no. 30, 1966).

29 C. Rawcliffe, *The Staffords, Earls of Stafford and Dukes of Buckingham* (Cambridge, Cambridge University Press, 1978).

30 R. Virgoe, 'The recovery of the Howards in East Anglia, 1485 to 1529', chapter I in *Wealth and Power in Tudor England* (see no. 13) – the earls of Oxford and Surrey.

31 B. Coward, *The Stanleys, Lords Stanley and Earls of Derby* (Chetham Society, Manchester, 3rd series, vol. 30, 1983).

32 P. Meredith (ed.), *Fulgens and Lucres, by Mayster Henry Medwall* (University of Leeds, School of English, 1981).

E. The later Tudors

33 P. Williams, *The Tudor Regime* (Oxford, Oxford University Press, 1979) – an admirable study which, although concentrating on Henry VIII and his successors, has much relevant material for Henry VII (use the index under 'Henry VII').

34 G. R. Elton, *Reform and Reformation: England 1509–1558* (Edward Arnold, 1977) – the most up-to-date account of Professor Elton's views, which have been somewhat modified in the light of recent research, as the footnotes bear witness.

F. Works published since 1985

Over the past ten years, much new work has been done on aspects of Henry VII's reign. Unfortunately, some of the most significant research (including the analysis of a large number of newly-discovered recognizances, many from the first years of the reign) is as yet unpublished; until it is, it cannot be incorporated into a brief general study such as this (though see no. 46, below). In the meantime, the following should be added to the revelant sections, above:

35 D. Starkey, *The Reign of Henry VIII*, chapters 1–2 (George Philip, 1985) – useful summary of Dr Starkey's research on Henry VII's inner household (§§B, E).

36   M. Bennett, *Lambert Simnel and the Battle of Stoke* (Gloucester, Alan Sutton, 1987) – stresses the importance of 1487 in Henry VII's reign (§B).

37   A. Goodman, *The New Monarchy: England 1471–1534* (Oxford, Basil Blackwell, 1988) – usefully complements this pamphlet (§A).

38   A. J. Pollard, *The Wars of the Roses* (Macmillan, 1988) – the best brief introduction to the wars (§C).

39   J. Guy, *Tudor England* (Oxford, Oxford University Press, 1988), chapters 1–3 – a solid if uninspiring account of the reign (§A).

40   T. B. Pugh, 'Henry VII and the English Nobility', in G. W. Bernard (ed.), *The Tudor Nobility* (Manchester, Manchester University Press, 1992) (§D).

41   M. K. Jones and M. Underwood, *The King's Mother: Lady Margaret Beaufort, Countess of Richmond and Derby* (Cambridge, Cambridge University Press, 1991) – the definitive study (§§B, D).

42   C. Carpenter, *Locality and Polity: A Study of Warwickshire Landed Society, 1401–1499* (Cambridge, Cambridge University Press, 1992), chapters 15–17 – arguing from the basis of massive research on Warwickshire that Henry was actually an incompetent king; an obviously challenging view, but one which to my mind is ultimately mistaken (§§B, D).

43   S. J. Gunn, 'The courtiers of Henry VII', *English Historical Review*, vol. 108 (1993) – a most important analysis (§D).

44   I. Arthurson, *The Perkin Warbeck Conspiracy, 1491–99* (Stroud, Alan Sutton, 1994) – demonstrates the seriousness of the Perkin Warbeck affair (§B).

45   S. J. Gunn, *Early Tudor Government, 1485–1558* (Basingstoke, Macmillan, 1995) – now the best study of this subject (§B).

46   S. Cunningham, 'Henry VII and Rebellion in Yorkshire, 1485–1492', to be published in *Northern History*, probably in 1996 – Henry's dealings with former supporters of Richard III: vital for understanding the initial establishment of the Tudor regime (§§B, D).